YOUR KNOWLEDGE HAS VALUE

Antje Holtmann

Language Contact

Zusammenfassung in Stichpunkten

GRIN Verlag

Bibliografische Information der Deutschen Nationalbibliothek:

Die Deutsche Bibliothek verzeichnet diese Publikation in der Deutschen National-
bibliografie; detaillierte bibliografische Daten sind im Internet über http://dnb.d-
nb.de/ abrufbar.

Imprint:

Copyright © 2014 GRIN Verlag GmbH
Druck und Bindung: Books on Demand GmbH, Norderstedt Germany
ISBN: 978-3-656-71224-4

This book at GRIN:

http://www.grin.com/en/e-book/277966/language-contact

GRIN - Your knowledge has value

Der GRIN Verlag publiziert seit 1998 wissenschaftliche Arbeiten von Studenten, Hochschullehrern und anderen Akademikern als eBook und gedrucktes Buch. Die Verlagswebsite www.grin.com ist die ideale Plattform zur Veröffentlichung von Hausarbeiten, Abschlussarbeiten, wissenschaftlichen Aufsätzen, Dissertationen und Fachbüchern.

Language Contact

- Historical development of language = gradual process of change → divergence
    - Speakers separated => development of dialects, separate languages
    - Linguistic families, mother and daughter languages
- Language contact + mixing
    - Footnote in historical linguistics
    - Gradual evolution and sudden change
    - No mother and daughter languages in interacting
- Language isolation = rare!
- Language contact
    - (occasionally) Divergence: maintain or increase linguistic differences
        - Desire to be different , purify language (no borrowing)
    - Convergence: shared features → mixing
        1. Maintain separation: only some borrowing (Arabic loans in Turkish and Farsi due to Islam), phonetically reshaped to fit, new sounds may arise, new word building techniques, only lexical borrowing
        2. High degree of bili: share grammar, e.g. Balkan Sprachbund
        3. Intermarriage: one group incorporated into another , more than lexical borrowing, imperfect learning → affects children → dialects (South America, Cherokee women married settlers)
        4. Language shift: abandon native language, interferences → ethnic dialect or new language, every time an immigrant learns new language and passes it on to children
            - segregation or more numerous than native speakers →abrupt creolization (learned conqueror's language → disease → natives pass on)
        5. need to communicate: lingua franca, official language, simplification/modification, e.g. koine
            - no time for learning → pidgin invented = makeshift mixture of different languages, economic reasons (trade), random combination or one language as base, culturally dominant language = supply vocab, grammar = mixture
                → not a complete language
                → if expanded => creolization
                → decreolization => minor dialect
- today: 200 creoles and pidgins
- language death = more common, but: substrate influence(Finnic tribes → Russian)

Handout Seminar

- language contact = confronted with different languages, influence each other
- scenarios
    - o war, trade, travel, intellectual life, new media
- factors
    - o domains, duration+intensity, power relations, prestige+attitude, competence bili
    - o structural similarities
- borrowing
    - o loanword: direct, whole sign (moprh. Importation)
    - o loanshift: indirect, concept adopted, expressed in RL (morph. substitution)
    - o loanblend: mixture of language
- intensive borrowing from Latin and French → triple structure
- direct borrowing
    - o hotline, homepage, check-in etc.
- indirect borrowing
    - o calques
        1. loan translation, "Wochenende" (exact)
        2. loan rendering, "Wolkenkratzer" (approximate)
        3. loan creation, "Nietenhose" (free substitution)
    - o semantic loans
        1. computer mouse → Maus
- hybrids (loanblend)
    - o combination engl+germ. Morphemes
    - o Haarspray, Popsänger
- Integration
    - o Phon., orthograph., morph. (gender,case,number)
- Pseudo-loans
    - o No equivalent in English
    - o Showmaster – quizmaster

S. Thomason

WHAT

- Use of more than 1 language same place same time → various situations
- BUT: def. language?
  - o Dialects, place (spread of Latin, Palin)
- Face-to-face interaction
- E.g. Switzerland: asymmetrical bili
- Existed as long as humanity has (Bible: Nehemia → intermarriage)
- Written or spoken?
- Language not in a vacuum/isolation → language contact as NORM
- Results
  - o Change → mostly borrowing
  - o Mixture → creoles, pidgins, bili
  - o Death → disease, attrition (overall change), force
- English up to 75% loans from French + Latin, after 1066 → evidence of close contact
- Not only words, all aspects of language can be borrowed, language structure (phon, morph, syn, lex)
- Absence of loanwords ≠ lack of contact

HOW

- European colonialization
- Alexander the Great: Greek → Indic
- Vikings: European → North America
- 16th century Spanish → Inca
- Cook: European → Pacific
- Onset not clear
  - o Two groups → unoccupied territory (not relevant anymore)
  - o Group → another group's territory (Native Am – Europeans)
- British Isles → successive immigration (military invasions)
  - o Immigration in general (German communities in USA)
  - o Importing labour force (slave trade, "involuntary" immigration)
  - o No Man's land
  - o Close cultural connection
  - o Education "learned contact" (Latin => diplomacy)

WHERE

- Social factors → stability
- Urbanization → against minority language
- Numbers of speakers, institutional support
- Language as symbol of ethnicity/loyalty
  - o Indigenous superordinate → no shift
  - o Migrant superordinate → might shift (Norman French)
  - o Indigenous subordinate → might shift slowly
  - o Migrant subordinate → shift rapidly

3

- English = lingua franca = contact
- Long-term peaceful relations = stable
- Conquest/invasion = least stable

Contact Explanations

- Cause of wide range of linguistic changes
- Historical linguists: diachronic (influence over time)
- Sociolinguists: synchronic (processes involved)
- Extreme positions
    o Contact as sole source for change
    o Only lexical chances and some structural
- Internal and external motivation
- Complexity of change processes
- What is language contact?
    o Some interaction of speakers with different languages
    o Face to face (mostly) => BUT: worldwide travel and communication today
    o Fluency in both languages
- What isn't language contact?
    o Internal explanation only
    o Difficult to find an isolated language
    o innovation of one or more speakers → Variation and change → spread/transfer
- Contact-induced change (change resulting from contact, but not based on that language)
    o a (multiple) source, less likely that it happened outside a specific contact situation
- no explanation for the vast majority of linguistic changes
    o too little information about social and linguistic circumstances in past situations
    o easy to find motivation for innovation, but combination of social and linguistic factors for success of failure too complex
    o goal: deeper understanding of processes, not predicting change
- establishment of internal and external factors
    o internal: learnability
    o external: difficult!
- Criteria for contact-induced change:
    o Consider recipient language (B) as a whole: transfer of only one structural feature is unlikely
    o Source language (A): prove contact
    o Shared features
    o Prove that feature is older in A, no innovation
    o Prove that feature is innovation in B (not existent before contact with A)
- Factors unique to c-i change, others shared with internal change, no clear cut
- Predicting that change can occur
    o Presence/absence of imperfect learning → major predictor
        ▪ Fluent speakers: first nonbasic vocab, later structural features and basic vocab
        ▪ Exception: communities avoiding lexical borrowing
        ▪ Shift-induced interference (imperfect learning): phon. + syntactic features predominant, lexical interference lags behind

4

- o Intensity of contact
  - Duration, level of bili in receiving language
  - More intensive = more likely to transfer structural features + lexical items
  - Shift: size of population speaking RL and SL, access to language, length of time
    - More shifting speakers, limited access, abrupt = large interference
    - E.g. Yiddish variety of English
    - Opposite: Norm French 1066-1200: outnumbered by English speakers, access unlimited, no abrupt shift → modest structural interference
  - Internally motivated change: spread of innovation person-to-person within speech community, social networks important (Milroy)
- o Speaker's attitude
  - Difficult to prove
  - Avoiding loanwords but not always consciously
  - Distinguish the language from others

Linguistic Predictors

- Typological distance
  - o Helps to predict kinds of interference
  - o Inflectional morph.
  - o Minimal distance = frequent interference, inflectional features
  - o Distance as barrier = difference of inflectional categories
  - o Any feature can be transferred => intense contact
- Universal markedness
  - o Ease of learning
    - drift: pattern pressure motivate change
    - burden on learning, diachronically unstable
  - o Hard to learn = hard to borrow
  - o Borrowing scales
  - o Evidence limited
  - o /t/ universal but /θ/ rare
  - o Less likely to adopt marked features
- Degree of integration into ling. System
  - o Inflections less likely transferred because tightly integrated, interlocking relationships
  - o Likely: nonbasic vocab, function words, phon. Confined to loans
  - o Inflectional morph. Least affected, highest degree of integration, very intense contact
- Need for ideal social conditions = strong cultural pressure from dominant language to transfer hard-to-learn features
- Attitude may favour adoption of innovations
- Internal and external factor have to be analyzed parallel
- Historical and sociolinguists have to work together

5

H. Hock

- Interlanguage - interference - transfer
- Code-switching
    - Switching back and forth
    - Syntax + morph.
- Code mixing
    - Lexical ($\cong$ lexical borrowing)
- → Mixed languages

Pidgins (fast, 2 generations)

- Structure simplification
- Radical reduction of vocabulary
- No passive, no inflection
- Lexicon 1000-2000 words

Creoles

- Process of expansion

J. Holm: Contact and Change

- Contacts → change
- 1980s development of contact ling.
- Pidgin and creole studies only in the second half of the 20th century

Pidgins

- Earliest known pidgin from 1068 CE
- Reduced language resulting from contact between groups with no common language
- Need of communication
- Group with less power: difficult work of learning vocab
- Group with more power: adopt changes in pronunciation, grammar, semantics → speak differently than with own group
- Emergency language
- Drop unnecessary things: inflection, reducing words, extend meaning
- Pidgin = restricted to limited use, no one's native language
- Languages distant from each other, social distance maintained

Creoles

- Earliest: 1671 Martinique (Caribbean)
- Settlement in 1635 → development of creole within 36 years
- Pidgin was first
- Creole = spoken as native language by whole community
    - Often displaced from original language (slavery)

6

- First generation => pidgin, next generation extended → creole
- Pidgin: less fluent, limited vocab, influence of mother tongue → massive variation
- Chaotic and incomplete input → organize it into creole
- Creolization = expansion (vs. reduction/pidginization)
- Phonol. Rules, complete vocabulary, innovative combination to fill gaps, reorganization of grammar
- Where do grammatical features come from? => various theories
- Decreolization: when creole is still in contact with donor language
- Continuum of varieties (differ in distance to superstrate)

Contact Linguistics

- Weinreich! 1953
- Much disagreement when defining object
- Since 1980s part of contact linguistics
- Increase understanding of possible outcomes of language contact
- Factors for selecting lexical or structural features: frequency, regularity, salience, transparency

P. Muysken: Scenarios for Language Contact
- languages not in a vacuum
- number of migrants, increase of multilingual communities
- mixed languages
- Dixon: equilibrium model questioned family tree model
- Discrepancy
  o Between historical linguistics and contemporary language contact studies
- Language chance = constrained by universals
- Kaufmann and Thomason against this view
- Nichols: stability of elements
  o Dimensions: Inherit, Borrow, Retain (shift), Select (pressure)
- Every change due to social AND structural causes

Borrowing:

- Spread of individual language items
- Words, morph. Elements, idiomatic meanings

D. Winford: Contact and Borrowing
- 2 vategories => Borrowing and interference/transfer
- borrowing: language maintenance
  o incorporation of foreign features into native language
  o any kind of transfer as result of contact
  o contact-induced transfer involving phonetic substance vs. transfer of meaning and syntax

- interference: L2 acquisition, language shift
  - o influence of L1 on L2
  - o subtype of borrowing ?
  - o non-deliberate transfer of ling. Features from L1 to L2
- Borrowing an imposition
  - o Transfer as neutral term for any influence
  - o Borrowing: RL speaker is agent, transfer of material, RL dominant
  - o Imposition: SL speaker is agent, using SL habits when speaking L2, SL dominant (RL less proficient)
- Linguistic dominance vs. social dominance
- Lexicon, derivational morph., free function morphemes = less stable = more amenable to change
- Phon., morph., syntax, semantics = more stable = less amenable to change
- Most often: lexicon
- No effect on grammar usually

Lexical Borrowing

- Classified since 19th century
- Betz: Lehnwort/loanword vs. Lehnprägung/loan coinage
- Lexical borrowings: loanwords, loan meanings, creations
  - o Loanwords: imitation of phon., meaning, pure loans ("burrito") and loan blends ("bossig")
  - o Loan meanings: change in semantics in RL
  - o Loan shifts: loan transfer, calques, word formation is replicated ("skyscraper") → "Wolkenkratzer")
  - o Creations: innovative use of native expressions to convey foreign concept
- Classification = description not process
- Borrowing = importation (adoption) and substitution (sounds or morphemes substituted for those in SL)
- Replaced by imitation and adaptation

Integration of Loanwords

- Adapted phon. + morph. of RL
  - o Epenthesis (addition of one or more sounds to a word)
  - o Syllabification of glides
  - o Cluster simplification
- Adapted to syntax and morph. in RL
  - o Case, number, gender
  - o In general few problems
    - Natural gender
    - Analogy determines gender
  - o English loan "Stress" m., as "Kampf" = semantically similar
- Borrowing => Close imitations, drastic change, inventions
- Often no complete adoption of foreign item, i.e. form and meaning
  - o New meanings

8

- o Foreign meaning for native lexeme
- o Innovations without counterpart in SL
- o Blends of native and foreign items
- Borrowed items manipulates => structural and semantic rules

Structural Elements

- Strict limits: what can be transferred, under which conditions
- Little evidence of direct transfer of phonemes, extremely rare
- Comes along with lexical borrowing
- Phonemic inventory may be changed: /s/ - /z/, /f/ - /v/
- Functional + grammatical elements
- Free functional elements borrowed directly
  - o Conjunctions, prepositions, pronouns
- Closed-class items less amenable to transfer
- Hierarchy of borrowing (Muysken) [confirmed in studies]
  - o Nouns – adj – verbs – a.s.o.
- Morph. can be borrowed
  - o Strict limits
  - o Bound derivational morphemes along with lexical b.
  - o Can become productive if en masse, e.g. French: -able, dis-
- Overt morph. borrowing very rare, through lexical borrowing
- Borrowing from Latin and Greek focus/foci etc.
  - o But only written, scholarly/few educated people
  - o Not productive
- Inflectional morphemes borrowed due to dialect/fit between languages
- Direct borrowing of structural elements = RARE

Constraints

- Social + ling.
- Social = prestige and need
  - o Borrowing from Native Am.
  - o Science, technology, higher learning
  - o Prestige: from French pork+beef for pig +cow
- Sociopolitical+sociolinguistic factors
  - o Social interaction, degree of bili, demographics, power relation, attitudes
  - o Social class and neighbourhood, education, social network etc.
  - o Language loyalty, ideology
    - ▪ Policies to Purify language
  - o Social mores and taboo may restrict borrowing
- Open-class borrowing = COMMON, because less stable/less cohesive, easier to isolate
- Typological distance as factor
- Higher degree of morph. complexity = resist b.
- B. facilitated if structure is congruent
- If verbal structure is barrier => compound verb: borrowed stem + native meaning
- Structural elements borrowed if congruence in morph. given

- Transparent morphemes → easier to isolate, clear meaning
- Gaps in morph. inventory → borrowing/importation in RL
- Little impact on overall grammar

Structural Patterns

- Borrowed quite regularly
- B. strictly only overt grammatical morph.
- Structural transfer = pattern transfer a.s.o.
- Traditional view => structural elements highly resistant
- Significant structural b. (Kaufmann+Thomason)
    o One language borrows entire grammar, keeping lexicon → mixed language
    o Long-term contact, gradual convergence → EXTREME
        ▪ Bakker against Kaufmann/Thomason
        ▪ Rather: massive lexical borrowing
        ▪ High degree of bili needed
        ▪ Borrowing (RL as agent) + imposition (SL as agent)
        ▪ Question of type and agentivity
- Many situations = ongoing shift → profiency → transfer
- Greek + Turkish in Asia Minor
    o Significant changes at all levels
    o Due to earlier b.
    o More proficient in Turkish → transfer + changes (new vowels etc.)
    o → beyond RL agentivity
- Distinguish agents of change and agentivity

Other Contact Phenomena

- Code-switching
    o Retaining morpho-syntactic frame of RL → importing morph./phrases from external SL
    o Inflection according to RL, open-class
    o Manifestation of b.
    o Start for mixed languages?
- Relexification
    o Process of vocab substitution, but only phonological representation
    o Lexical forms from SL imported, unchanged RL structural frame
- Creation of mixed languages
    o 3 layers: affixes, number/pronouns, markers/morph.
    o Conscious act of "folk linguistic engineering" → signal of identity
- Borrowing → range of outcomes
- RL agentivity

Contact I (R. Mesthrie)

Contact and Borrowing
- Def.
    - o Incorporation of an item from one language into another
    - o Words, grammatical elements, sounds
    - o Adaption of a word into phonemic and grammatical system
    - o Does not require knowledge of language (vs. code-switching!)
    - o Stays in the RL, no intention of returning it
    - o Word stays in SL
- Sociolinguists = cultural aspects of b., learning/acculturation

Language Maintenance
- "Shift" by Weinreich first, 1953
    - o Change from the habitual use of one language to that of another
- Maintenance and shift by Fishman, 1964
    - o M. = continuing use of a language in the face of competition from a regionally and socially more powerful language
    - o S. = replacement of the language, means of communication
    - o Death = community is the last one to speak a language
- Shift studied by Nancy Dorian
    - o Oberwart/Austria: Hungarian → German
- Shift without death
- Death without shift
- Types of death
    - o Gradual: replacement (Gaelic → English)
    - o Sudden: rapid distinction without bili period, monolingual
    - o Radical: repression, fluent speakers but no transmission
    - o Bottom-to-top: only special use, e.g. religion, songs
- Causes of shift
- ➔ No single set of factors
    - o higher education in dominant language ⌐
    - o Number of speakers in dominant language ⌐ Kloss
    - o Similarity between languages
    - o Attitudes of dominant language ⌐
    - o Economic factors (immigration, trade, industrialization) ⌐
    - o Demographic factors (number and distribution of speakers) ⌐ Appel/Muysken
    - o Institutional support (use in education, media) ⌐
- Course of shift
    - o Bili period
    - o Specific domains of languages
        - ▪ Public/formal = dominant language
        - ▪ Informal/personal = minority language
    - o Progressive redistribution (home, religion last)

- More than one minority weaken each other → Need of lingua franca = dominat language (English)
- Cases where minority gives up language (e.g. Saami)
- Speaker competence
  - Young fluent: fluent but deviation from older speakers
  - Passive bilis: understand but not productive
  - Semi-speakers: flawed speaking but usage
- 1490-1990 half of languages died
- 5000-6000 languages today, various stages
- 90% of them will die (Krauss) if nothing is done
- Question of power politics rather than linguistic structure

Contact II (Mesthrie)

Creoles and Pdigins
- New codes arising from the realignment of people from different linguistic traditions

Pidgin

- Languages in contact without lingua franca
- Rapid need of communications → simple type of language
- May draw on languages involved
- Not a 2nd language learning
- Signs of language mixing
- Not a first language
- But: own rules and norms of usage
- Differences in grammatical structures
  - Jargon/pre-pidgin: unstable, limited vocab
  - Stable p.: recognizable structure, developed vocab, limited to certain domains
  - Expanded p.: level of sophistication, many contexts
  - Creoles: developed from p., first language
- Historical background
  - Slave trade
  - Colonialization
  - Trade
  - War
  - Labour migration

- Vocabulary
  - Small
  - Polysemy: one word carriers several meanings
  - Multifunctional: different grammatical uses (e.g. noun+adj.)
  - Circumlocution: paraphrasing
  - Compounding

- Grammar
  - Few suffixes, grammatical markers
  - Tense from context or adverbs
  - Same stable pidgin have suffixes
- Origin
  - Several theories → similarities of pidgins
  - Monogenesis
    - 1960s, derived from Portuguese (=earliest explorers, formed basis, vocab replaced later = relexification)
  - Independent parallel development
    - Parallel circumstances => parallel outcomes
    - European languages = similar in structure
    - Colonies = same group of languages
    - "Foreigner talk" → slaves had no access to real language
  - Linguistic universals
    - Inherent linguistic skills of all humans

Creoles

- Creolisation = expansion of pidgin
- Covers all aspects
  - Vocab expanded
  - Phono. Rules
  - Coherent verbal system, tense, markers etc.
- Theories
  - Bioprogramme
  - Gradualism
  - Decreolization
    - Access to superstrate language → change
      - Basilect: most remote from prestige language
      - Acrolect: superstrate language
      - Mesolect: intermediate
- Recreolisation

New English Varieties

- Where ENgish is not spoken as 1st language
- Education system
- Range of funtions
- Indigenized by adopting words from local culture
- → Nativisation

Code-Switching (Mesthrie)

- Language varieties = associations by speakers/listeners
- CAT
    - Converge/adopt: reduce social distance
    - Diverge (speak differently): emphasize distinctiveness
    - overaccommadation
- Accommodation = specific motivations for adopting, general phenomenon (moni, bili)
- Domains
    - Patterns of language choice depend on social background
    - Habitual language choice
    - Patterns of language use
- Bili communities => stable, but possibility of language shift or death
- Li Wei, types
    - Between conversational turns (different levels of ability/attitudes)
    - Within a speaking turn, at sentence boundary
    - Switching between constituents in a sentence (intra-sentential)
- 1972 > interest begins, influential study of bidialectal community in Norway
    - Local dialect (Ranamaal) and standard variety (Bokmaal) (Hemnesberget)
    - Linguistically similar, but distinct entities
    - Different social functions
    - Dialect = local cultural identiy (home, family)
    - Standard = formal education
    - Used in different occasions, but also switch during an event
    - Convey certain social meanings → since then studied by many researchers
    - Oberwart, Austria by Gal, 1979
- Unmarked choice => expected in the context
- Marked choice => language use not expected
- Myers-Scotton: markedness model
    - Series of UC between different languages: change of topic → other variety more appropriate
    - CS as UC itself → no meaning of switch, both languages meaningful
    - CS as marked choice → not conform to expected patterns, increase social distance, express authority
    - CS as exploratory choice → when UC is uncertain, little knowledge of social identiy
- CS is meaningful
- Choice → maintaining social identity, CS = different identities
- Particular switches =meaningful, act of CS
- Unmarked/expected choice
- Marked/unexpected choice => imitate a change to relationship
- CS = useful in cases of uncertainty of relationships, negotiate identities
- Auer = conversational analysis vs. Myers-Scotton = social interpretation
- → combine sequential and social meaning, e.g. Gal
- CS study = language use of individual, aspects of identity, contexts → similar to mono stylistic variation (quantitative)
- CS: generalizations about patterns → Qualitative approach

Code-Switching (Myers-Scotton)

- Discourse with morphemes from two or more of the varieties in their linguistic repertoire
- Most researchers → Main reason = lack of sufficient proficiency in the opening language
- Choice of language for all words is not free!
- Between languages, dialects, styles, registers
- Early studies: social functions, strategy for influencing interpersonal relationships
- Contextualization cue, signaling and interpreting speaker intentions
- Micro-level studies
- Strategy of neutrality
- Who uses what linguistic varieties where and to whom?
- Depends on linguistic repertoire and demographic factors (e.g. education)
- Social class, proficiency, attitudes but: norms of community override individual
- Intrasentential switching
    o Where in a sentence can a speaker change languages?
- Involves total change, also phonology
- CS = "Empirical window"
    o Bilingual speech production, nature of linguistic competence
- Social and discourse motivations
- Dynamics of intergroup relations
- Interaction of bili proficiency and attitudes

Structure

- Matrix Language ML and Embedded Language EL
- ML => grammatical frame
- Mixed constituents
- Aware of differential participation of the languages in CS
- Intrasentential and intersentential
- ML
    o Contributing more morphemes

Bilingual Speech

- Proficient bili speakers engage in CS
- More ability in one language
- Predictable structures
    o Grammatical frame = ML
- Motivations distinguish CS from others
    o Add a dimension to the socio-pragmatic force
        ▪ Individual lexical choices
    o Discourse marker
    o Convey intentions → lexicalize semantic/pragmatic features from EL (mismatch in ML)
    o Features only in EL (lexical gap in ML)
- Selection of mode, below consciousness
- Cases of **language attrition**

- o Waning ability in one language
- o Losing consistency in producing grammatical frames or lexemes
- Coincides with CS
  - o Still setting gram. Frame → gradual turnover in ML
  - o Proficient enough in both languages
- 1st language attrition → immigration, 2nd generation = shift
- **Creoles/pidgins akin with CS**
  - o Attempting to structure utterances following a grammatical frame which they do not yet have full command of
  - o Inability to express all intentions in one language
- CS ≠ **borrowing**
  - o Similar, often identical
  - o Related in motivations
  - o Elements from one language are inserted into the grammatical frame of another
  - o Monolinguals can borrow
  - o Only bili can do CS
  - o Lexemes from more sociopolitical dominant language are borrowed into less commanding language
  - o Direction of b., types of words, types of speakers

Contact Phenomena

- **Convergence**
  - o Similar to attrition
  - o Rearrangement of how grammatical frames are projected under influence of another language
  - o Structural simplification may accompany (=>attrition)
  - o High sentiment to maintain the language, Numerous speakers →← dominant language
  - o Maintained languages in spite of convergence (German communities in the USA)
  - o Modification of one gram. Frame, no turnover
- Mixed languages
  - o Shift beginning with turnover to ML but incomplete

Sociolinguistics

- Markedness Model → language choice free ← objected by many researchers!
  - o Unmarked choice (not the language of higher prestige)
- CS = in-group mode of communication
- One languages contributes more material
- Social conditions (direction of CS)
- Aspect of prominence
- CS = emblematic of dual membership

Conclusion

- Two stands in research
  - o Old: Discourse-organizing messages of CS

- o   Current: reflection of group's attitudes, morphosyntax
- Broader views: Bili speech production, competence, relation to other contact phenomena

Code switching (Gardner-Chloros)

- CS = use of several languages or dialects in the same conversation or sentence by bili people
- Affects everybody who is in contact with languages
- Occurs alongside of other contact phenomena (b., pid., death, convergence)
- Expressing group identity
- Main approaches
  - o   Sociolinguistics
  - o   Pragmatics
  - o   Grammatical analysis/underlying rules
- Terminology is very much discussed!
- Distinguishable from borrowing? Code-mixing?
- Working definitions needed
  - o   Alternation of 2 languages in conversation
  - o   Code = languages, dialects and so on (BUT: originally communication tech.)
  - o   Switching = alternation
- Haugen (one of the first writers)
  - o   Code-switching-Interference-Integration
- Why CS occurs
  - o   Laziness (easy option when word is missing)
  - o   Attitude (speakers disapprove of CS)
  - o   Awareness (below consciousness)
- CS =
  - o   each time minority language groups come into contact with majority language groups, rapid social change OR
  - o   Feature of stable bili
- Little or no prominence in studies
- CS = spoken genre, but also written texts, from various historical periods
- Informality of conversation (email)

Tendencies

- Bringing varieties together – what extent? (convergence/divergence)
- Principal mechanism of borrowing
- No result of "imperfect learning"
- Important component of change
- Middle English → relexified under Norman French and Latin influence
  - o   Relexification = process by which a language replaces part or all of its lexical stock with words from another variety while keeping its basic grammatical identity
- CS occurs with varying stability
- CS stage (point in sentence where the switch appears) → Language mixing (unmarked choice, overall switching mode) → fused lects (stabilized mixed varieties)

- Juxtaposition of 2 languages perceived and interpreted as locally meaningful by participants (Auer)
- CS = insider activity
- Popular singers use CS

Language interaction

- CS as source of borrowing
- Role in contact = matter of discussion
- B. = commonest kind of CS
- Any aspect can be borrowed
- Common nouns most frequently b.
    o Freer of syntactic relation
    o Accessible at any level of bili
- Loans start as CS → then generalize among speakers → integration
- Presence/absence of CS = prestige of pidgin
    o Prestige low = CS

Structural and social influence

- Outcomes of contact
    o B. = affects both the influenced and influencing variety
    o Interference through shift = sounds, syntax, morph.
- Social context!
- No universal rules
- Imbalance in power/status between groups in contact → CS reflects this => asymmetrical
- CS = one outcome of contact, co-occurring with others
    o Neglected/ignored in studies
- Social level = product of power struggle
- Individual level = bili competences, discourse-structuring

Disglossia

- Two dialects or closely related languages are used by one community

Language Contact (Appel/Muysken)

Language Maintenance and Shift
- Bili communities
- Dominant language takes over domains
- E.g. Cornish
- Shift = neutral (not necessarily towards majority lang, e.g. French in Canada)
- Language is reduced → language loss, language death
- Factors
  - Economic/socio/language status
    - Prominent factor
    - E.g. Spanish in the USA (spoken by poor people/English = academic)
  - Demographic
    - Geographical distribution
    - Concentrated = maintenance (French in Quebec)
  - Institutional support
    - Government, church, organizations etc.
    - Mass media (TV and radio)
    - Education (proficiency fostered)
- Vitality of linguistic group = maintenance
- Language behavior + attitudes
- Susan Gal, Oberwart study
  - Economic changes: industrialization
  - Language and identity
    - Express social status
  - Social networks
    - Informal/formal interaction
- Gradual change
  - Language A and B are used, then B = categorical
- Question of generation
- Changing social situations => faster shift (e.g. immigration)
  - 1. Generation = bili (minority dominant)
  - 2. Generation = bili (either)
  - 3. Generation = bili (majority dominant)
  - 4. Generation = mono, majority language
- Language loss
  - Loss of territory → less proficiency
  - Loss of lexical skills → relexification (words are replaced)
  - Reduction of morph. system, simplified, only general rules
    - E.g. Gaelic: suffixation
  - Monostylism
    - Reduction of stylistic variants → used in fewer situation
  - Loss of identity
  - Shift + loss = hand in hand

Code-switching

-   Sociolinguistics: why?
-   Pyscholing: capacity to switch?
-   Linguistics: really switching?
-   No isolated phenomenon
-   Types
    o   Tag-switches (emblematic switch, Poplack)
    o   Intra-sentential (code-mixing, in the middle of the sentence)
    o   Inter-sentitial
    → mostly generalized
-   Why switch?
    o   Reference: lack of knowledge in one language, consciously
    o   Direction: e.g. excluding people from the conversation
    o   Expression: emphasis on mixed identity
    o   Phatic: change in tone, highlight information
    o   Metalinguistic: commenting on the languages
    o   Poetic
-   Only fully bili speakers, certain proficiency (from age 8)
-   But: including words also on lower level
-   Where switch?
    o   Grammatical constraints
    o   Universal c.
        ▪   Linearity: parallel word-order → switch possible
        ▪   Dependency: no switch between 2 elements if lexical dependent, grammatical independence needed
    o   Externally/internally (triggering) conditioned switching
    o   Relativized c.
        ▪   More languages involved
        ▪   Word phonologically similar
        ▪   Morpheme for nativization

Language Contact and Change

-   No consensus on borrowing
-   What is language?
    o   System: tightly organized wholes, all elements related, complex syntax/pragmatics (Sassure)
    o   Bag of tricks: compex tools, easy adaption (Schuchardt)
-   What can be borrowed? In focus, not process of b./contact situations
-   Lexical b. = acknowledged by all researchers
-   Scenarios of grammatical b.
    o   Convergence: on phonetic level, several languages in the same area by the same people
    o   Cultural influence (lexical b.)
    o   Relexification: not always possible to maintain grammar, new function words
    o   2nd Language learning: interference with 1st language
    o   Imitation of prestige patterns

Lexical Borrowing
- Linguistic purism widespread

Typology

- Haugen: importation (foreign pattern) and substitution (native pattern)
    - Loanwords: most common, importation "chic"
    - Loan blends: importation + substitution (hybrids) "soft-ware huis"
    - Loan shifts: importation of meaning "Wolkenkratzer"
- Albo: substitution and addition
- Core and non-core vocabulary

Determinants

- Weinreich
    - Cultural influence
    - Rare native words are replaced
    - Need for synonyms
    - New semantic distinctions
    - Intensive bili
- Loans in English
    - Norse Vikings and Danes (8-11th cent.)
    - French Vikings (11th cent.)
    - Latin (conversion to Christianity, 6th cent.)

Grammatical constraints

- Nouns are easiest to borrow
- Different hierarchies, types not tokens
- Extend referential function of language

Difference to code-mixing

- CM = non-native items not adapted in morph. and phon.
    - BUT: different degree of phon. adaptation of borrowed word
- Integration = very gradual → degree indicated time of borrowing
- Frequency of use, displacements of native synonyms, gramm. Integration, acceptability

Language death

- Without implications, or sign of attrition
- Lack of variation, not amount of b.

Pidgins and Creoles

- Pidgin = strongly reduced linguistic system, no native language
- Creole = emerged from pidgin, acquired as native language
- Jargon (involves migration of group), forced to develop new communication system
- Vocabulary from dominant language → most pidgins from European languages
- Creoles might emerge when pidgin is only linguistic model
  - Creole remains
  - Creole loses status
  - Creole develops towards dominant language
- Pidgins – Africa, Pacific Ocean
- Creoles – Caribbean, West Africa, Indian Ocean, Far East
- Former: historical linguistics, now: centre of research
- Creoles are
  - More alike than other languages
  - More simple
  - More mixed grammars
    - Semantic transparency: universal
    - Imperfect 2nd language learning: simplification
    - Baby-talk: simplified input
    - Portuguese mono-genesis: language of trade, slaves learned jargon
    - Bio-program: innate linguistic capacity → fully-fledged language